BLUETS

张清物
Ashley Zhang.

2018.3.7
购于The Strand

大雪.

WAVE BOOKS   SEATTLE AND NEW YORK

MAGGIE NELSON   BLUETS

PUBLISHED BY WAVE BOOKS

WWW.WAVEPOETRY.COM

WAVE BOOKS TITLES ARE DISTRIBUTED

TO THE TRADE BY CONSORTIUM

BOOK SALES AND DISTRIBUTION

PHONE: 800-283-3572 / SAN 631-760X

THIS TITLE IS AVAILABLE IN

LIMITED EDITION HARDCOVER

DIRECTLY FROM THE PUBLISHER

LIBRARY OF CONGRESS

CATALOGING-IN-PUBLICATION DATA

NELSON, MAGGIE, 1973–

BLUETS / MAGGIE NELSON. — 1ST ED.

P. CM.

ISBN 978-1-933517-40-7 (PBK. : ALK. PAPER)

I. TITLE.

PS3564.E4687B56 2009

811′.54—DC22

2009005830

DESIGNED AND COMPOSED BY QUEMADURA

PRINTED IN THE UNITED STATES OF AMERICA

14 13 12 11 10 9

WAVE BOOKS 020

BLUETS

And were it true, we do not think all philosophy is worth one hour of pain. PASCAL, *Pensées*

1. Suppose I were to begin by saying that I had fallen in love with a color. Suppose I were to speak this as though it were a confession; suppose I shredded my napkin as we spoke. *It began slowly. An appreciation, an affinity. Then, one day, it became more serious. Then* (looking into an empty teacup, its bottom stained with thin brown excrement coiled into the shape of a sea horse) *it became somehow* personal.

2. And so I fell in love with a color—in this case, the color blue—as if falling under a spell, a spell I fought to stay under and get out from under, in turns.

change of perspective
suppose
⇒ scene.
(confession)

(love):
do I want
to stay or
leave?

3. Well, and what of it? A voluntary delusion, you might say. That each blue object could be a kind of burning bush, a secret code meant for a single agent, an X on a map too diffuse ever to be unfolded in entirety but that contains the knowable universe. How could all the shreds of blue garbage bags stuck in brambles, or the bright blue tarps flapping over every shanty and fish stand in the world, be, in essence, the fingerprints of God? *I will try to explain this.*

4. I admit that I may have been lonely. I know that loneliness can produce bolts of hot pain, a pain which, if it stays hot enough for long enough, can begin to simulate, or to provoke—take your pick—an apprehension of the divine. (*This ought to arouse our suspicions.*)

5. But first, let us consider a sort of case in reverse. In 1867, after a long bout of solitude, the French poet Stéphane Mallarmé wrote to his friend Henri Cazalis: "These last months have been terrifying. My Thought has thought itself through and reached a Pure Idea. What the rest of me has suffered during that long agony, is in-

describable." Mallarmé described this agony as a battle that took place on God's "boney wing." "I struggled with that creature of ancient and evil plumage—God—whom I fortunately defeated and threw to earth," he told Cazalis with exhausted satisfaction. Eventually Mallarmé began replacing "le ciel" with "l'Azur" in his poems, in an effort to rinse references to the sky of religious connotations. "Fortunately," he wrote Cazalis, "I am quite dead now."

6. The half-circle of blinding turquoise ocean is this love's primal scene. That this blue exists makes my life a remarkable one, just to have seen it. To have seen such beautiful things. To find oneself placed in their midst. Choiceless. I returned there yesterday and stood again upon the mountain. *[handwritten: love rather life]*

[handwritten: author herself? / reader?]

7. But kind of love is it, really? Don't fool yourself and call it sublimity. Admit that you have stood in front of a little pile of powdered ultramarine pigment in a glass cup at a museum and felt a stinging desire. But to do what? Liberate it? Purchase it? Ingest it? There is so little blue food in nature—in fact blue in the wild tends to

mark food to avoid (mold, poisonous berries)—that culinary advisers generally recommend against blue light, blue paint, and blue plates when and where serving food. But while the color may sap appetite in the most literal sense, it feeds it in others. You might want to reach out and disturb the pile of pigment, for example, first staining your fingers with it, then staining the world. You might want to dilute it and swim in it, you might want to rouge your nipples with it, you might want to paint a virgin's robe with it. But still you wouldn't be accessing the blue of it. Not exactly.

8. Do not, however, make the mistake of thinking that all desire is yearning. "We love to contemplate blue, not because it advances to us, but because it draws us after it," wrote Goethe, and perhaps he is right. But I am not interested in longing to live in a world in which I already live. I don't want to yearn for blue things, and God forbid for any "blueness." Above all, I want to stop missing you.

9. So please do not write to tell me about any more beautiful blue things. To be fair, this book will not tell you

about any, either. It will not say, *Isn't X beautiful?* Such demands are murderous to beauty.

10. The most I want to do is show you the end of my index finger. Its muteness.

11. That is to say: I don't care if it's colorless.

12. And please don't talk to me about "things as they are" being changed upon any "blue guitar." What can be changed upon a blue guitar is not of interest here.

13. At a job interview at a university, three men sitting across from me at a table. On my CV it says that I am currently working on a book about the color blue. I have been saying this for years without writing a word. It is, perhaps, my way of making my life feel "in progress" rather than a sleeve of ash falling off a lit cigarette. One of the men asks, *Why blue?* People ask me this question often. I never know how to respond. We don't get to choose what or whom we love, I want to say. We just don't get to choose.

14. I have enjoyed telling people that I am writing a book about blue without actually doing it. Mostly what happens in such cases is that people give you stories or leads or gifts, and then you can play with these things instead of with words. Over the past decade I have been given blue inks, paintings, postcards, dyes, bracelets, rocks, precious stones, watercolors, pigments, paperweights, goblets, and candies. I have been introduced to a man who had one of his front teeth replaced with lapis lazuli, solely because he loved the stone, and to another who worships blue so devoutly that he refuses to eat blue food and grows only blue and white flowers in his garden, which surrounds the blue ex-cathedral in which he lives. I have met a man who is the primary grower of organic indigo in the world, and another who sings Joni Mitchell's *Blue* in heartbreaking drag, and another with the face of a derelict whose eyes literally leaked blue, and I called this one the prince of blue, which was, in fact, his name.

15. I think of these people as my blue correspondents, whose job it is to send me blue reports from the field.

16. But you talk of all this jauntily, when really it is more like you have been mortally ill, and these correspondents send pieces of blue news as if last-ditch hopes for a cure.

17. But what goes on in you when you talk about color as if it were a cure, when you have not yet stated your disease.

18. A warm afternoon in early spring, New York City. We went to the Chelsea Hotel to fuck. Afterward, from the window of our room, I watched a blue tarp on a roof across the way flap in the wind. You slept, so it was my secret. It was a smear of the quotidian, a bright blue flake amidst all the dank providence. It was the only time I came. It was essentially our lives. It was shaking.

19. Months before this afternoon I had a dream, and in this dream an angel came and said: *You must spend more time thinking about the divine, and less time imagining unbuttoning the prince of blue's pants at the Chelsea Ho-*

tel. But what if the prince of blue's unbuttoned pants *are* the divine, I pleaded. *So be it,* she said, and left me to sob with my face against the blue slate floor.

language!
actual move

20. *Fucking leaves everything as it is. Fucking may in no way interfere with the actual use of language. For it cannot give it any foundation either. It leaves everything as it is.*

21. Different dream, same period: Out at a house by the shore, a serious landscape. There was a dance underway, in a mahogany ballroom, where we were dancing the way people dance when they are telling each other how they want to make love. Afterward it was time for rough magic: to cast the spell I had to place each blue object (two marbles, a miniature feather, a shard of azure glass, a string of lapis) into my mouth, then hold them there while they discharged an unbearable milk. When I looked up you were escaping on a skiff, suddenly wanted. I spit out the objects in a snaky blue paste on my plate and offered to help the police boat look for you, but they said the currents were too unusual. So I stayed behind, and became

known as the lady who waits, the sad sack of town with hair that smells like an animal.

22. Some things do change, however. A membrane can simply rip off your life, like a skin of congealed paint torn off the top of a can. I remember that day very clearly: I had received a phone call. A friend had been in an accident. Perhaps she would not live. She had very little face, and her spine was broken in two places. She had not yet moved; the doctor described her as "a pebble in water." I walked around Brooklyn and noticed that the faded periwinkle of the abandoned Mobil gas station on the corner was suddenly blooming. In the baby-shit yellow showers at my gym, where snow sometimes fluttered in through the cracked gated windows, I noticed that the yellow paint was peeling in spots, and a decent, industrial blue was trying to creep in. At the bottom of the swimming pool, I watched the white winter light spangle the cloudy blue and I knew together they made God. When I walked into my friend's hospital room, her eyes were a piercing, pale blue and the only part of her body that could move. I was scared. So was she. The blue was beating.

23. Goethe wrote *Theory of Colours* in a period of his life described by one critic as "a long interval, marked by nothing of distinguished note." Goethe himself describes the period as one in which "a quiet, collected state of mind was out of the question." Goethe is not alone in turning to color at a particularly fraught moment. Think of filmmaker Derek Jarman, who wrote his book *Chroma* as he was going blind and dying of AIDS, a death he also forecast on film as disappearing into a "blue screen." Or of Wittgenstein, who wrote his *Remarks on Colour* during the last eighteen months of his life, while dying of stomach cancer. He knew he was dying; he could have chosen to work on any philosophical problem under the sun. He chose to write about color. About color and pain. Much of this writing is urgent, opaque, and uncharacteristically boring. "That which I am writing about so tediously, may be obvious to someone whose mind is less decrepit," he wrote.

24. "In view of the fact that Goethe's explanation of color makes no physical sense at all," one critic recently noted, "one might wonder why it is considered appropriate to

reissue this English translation." Wittgenstein put it this way: "This much I understand: that a physical theory (such as Newton's) cannot solve the problems that motivated Goethe, even if he himself didn't solve them either." So what were Goethe's problems?

25. Goethe was interested in the case of "a lady, who, after a fall by which an eye was bruised, saw all objects, but especially white objects, glittering in colours, even to an intolerable degree." This story is but one of many Goethe relates of people whose vision has been injured or altered and who seemingly never heal, even when the cause of the injury is psychological or emotional in nature. "This indicates extreme weakness of the organ, its inability to recover itself," he observes.

26. After my friend's accident, I began to think of this lady of the bruised eye and these glittering white objects with more frequency. Could such a phenomenon be happening to me, with blue, by proxy? I've heard that a diminishment of color vision often accompanies depression, though I do not have any idea how or why such a

thing is neurologically possible. So what would it be a symptom of, to start seeing colors—or, more oddly, just one color—more acutely? Mania? Monomania? Hypomania? Shock? Love? Grief?

27. But why bother with diagnoses at all, if a diagnosis is but *a restatement of the problem?*

28. It was around this time that I first had the thought: we fuck well because he is a passive top and I am an active bottom. I never said this out loud, but I thought it often. I had no idea how true it would prove, or how painful, outside of the fucking.

29. If a color cannot cure, can it at least incite hope? The blue collage you sent me so long ago from Africa, for example, made me hopeful. But not, to be honest, because of its blues.

because of you.

30. If a color could deliver hope, does it follow that it could also bring despair? I can think of many occasions on which a blue has made me feel suddenly hopeful (turning one's car around a sharp curve on a precipice and

abruptly finding ocean; flipping on the light in a stranger's bathroom one presumed to be white but which was, in fact, robin-egg blue; coming across a collection of navy blue bottle tops pressed into cement on the Williamsburg Bridge, or a shining mountain of broken blue glass outside a glass factory in Mexico), but for the moment, I can't think of any times that blue has caused me to despair.

31. Consider the case of Mr. Sidney Bradford, however, whose corneal opacities were grafted away at the age of fifty-two. After his vision was restored, he became unexpectedly disconsolate. "He found the world drab, and was upset by flaking paint and other blemishes; he liked bright colours, but became depressed when they faded." Not long after he gained vision and saw the world in full color, he "died in unhappiness."

32. When I say "hope," I don't mean hope for anything in particular. I guess I just mean thinking that it's worth it to keep one's eyes open. "What are all those / fuzzy-looking things out there? / Trees? Well, I'm tired / of them": the last words of William Carlos Williams's English grandmother.

33. I must admit that not all blues thrill me. I am not overly interested in the matte stone of turquoise, for example, and a tepid, faded indigo usually leaves me cold. Sometimes I worry that if I am not moved by a blue thing, I may be completely despaired, or dead. At times I fake my enthusiasm. At others, I fear I am incapable of communicating the depth of it.

34. *Acyanoblepsia:* non-perception of blue. A tier of hell, to be sure—albeit one that could be potentially corrected by Viagra, one of whose side effects is to see the world tinged with blue. The expert on guppy menopause, whose office is across from mine at the Institute, tells me this. He says it has something to do with a protein in the penis that bears a similarity to a protein in the retina, but beyond that I cannot follow.

35. Does the world look bluer from blue eyes? Probably *self-attacking* not, but I choose to think so (self-aggrandizement).

36. Goethe describes blue as a lively color, but one devoid of gladness. "It may be said to disturb rather than en-

liven." Is to be in love with blue, then, to be in love with a disturbance? Or is the love itself the disturbance? And what kind of madness is it anyway, to be in love with something constitutionally incapable of loving you back?

love the blue. love you.

37. Are you sure—one would like to ask—that it cannot love you back?

38. For no one really knows what color is, where it is, even whether it is. (*Can it die? Does it have a heart?*) Think of a honeybee, for instance, flying into the folds of a poppy: it sees a gaping violet mouth, where we see an orange flower and assume that it's orange, that we're normal.

39. The Encyclopedia does not help. "If normally our perception of color involves 'false consciousness,' what is the right way to think of colors?" it asks. "In the case of color, unlike other cases," it concludes, "false consciousness should be a cause for celebration."

40. When I talk about color and hope, or color and despair, I am not talking about the red of a stoplight, a peri-

winkle line on the white felt oval of a pregnancy test, or a black sail strung from a ship's mast. I am trying to talk about what blue means, or what it means to me, apart from meaning.

[handwritten margin note: not about the conventional symbolism & metaphore.]
[handwritten note: " meaning apart from meaning"]

41. On the eve of the millennium, driving through the Valley of the Moon. On the radio a DJ was going through the best albums of the century, and somewhere, I think around number thirty, was Joni Mitchell's *Blue*. The DJ played "River," and said that its greatness lies in the fact that no woman had ever said it so clearly and unapologetically before: *I'm so hard to handle, I'm selfish and I'm sad.* Progress! I thought. Then came the song's next line: *Now I've gone and lost the best baby that I ever had.*

[handwritten margin note: bravely state oneself]
[handwritten margin note: apology feel sorry]

42. Sitting in my office before teaching a class on prosody, trying not to think about you, about my having lost you. *But how can it be? How can it be? Was I too blue for you. Was I too blue.* I look down at my lecture notes: Heárt-bréak *is a spondee.* Then I lay my head down on the desk and start to weep. —*Why doesn't this help?*

43. Before a faculty meeting, talking again with the expert on guppy menopause. *What do biologists make of the question, Does color exist?* I ask. Duh, he says. A male guppy looking for a mate doesn't worry about whether color exists, he says. A male guppy only cares about being orange, in order to attract one. *But can it really be said that the guppy cares about being orange?* I ask. No, he admits. The male guppy simply *is* orange. *Why orange?* I ask. He shrugs. In the face of some questions, he says, biologists can only vacate the field.

44. This particular conversation with the expert on guppy menopause takes place on a day when, later that afternoon, a therapist will say to me, *If he hadn't lied to you, he would have been a different person than he is.* She is trying to get me to see that although I thought I loved this man very completely for exactly who he was, I was in fact blind to the man he actually was, or is.

I love a lie.

45. This pains me enormously. She presses me to say why; I can't answer. Instead I say something about how clinical

love is unexplicable.

psychology forces everything we call love into the patho-
logical or the delusional or the biologically explicable, that
if what I was feeling wasn't love then I am forced to admit
that I don't know what love is, or, more simply, that I loved
a bad man. How all of these formulations drain the blue
right out of love and leave an ugly, pigmentless fish flapping on a cutting board on a kitchen counter.

46. *Disavowal,* says the silence.

47. *Is there a good kind of hustler?* I wonder, as I steer my
car through the forest of gargantuan billboards, ghostly
palm trees, and light-flattened boulevards that have become my life.

48. Imagine, for example, someone who fucks like a
whore. Someone who seems good at it, professional.
Someone you can still see fucking you, in the mirror, always in the mirror, crazy fucking about three feet away, in
an apartment lit by blue light, never lit by daylight, this
person is always fucking you from behind in blue light and
you both always seem good at it, dedicated and lost unto

it, as if there is no other activity on God's given earth your bodies know how to do except fuck and be fucked like this, in this dim blue light, in this mirror. What do you call someone who fucks this way?

49. There is a color inside of the fucking, but it is not blue.

50. The confusion about what color is, where it is, or whether it is persists despite thousands of years of prodding at the phenomenon. And literally prodding: in his zeal, in the "dark chamber" of his room at Trinity College, Newton at times took to sticking iron rods or sticks in his eyes to produce then analyze his perceptions of color. Children whose vision has been damaged have been known to smash their fingers into their eyes to recreate color sensations that have been lost to them. (*That's the spirit!*)

51. *You might as well act* as if *objects had the colors,* the Encyclopedia says. —Well, it is as you please. But what would it look like to act otherwise?

52. Try, if you can, not to talk as if colors emanated from a single physical phenomenon. Keep in mind the effects of all the various surfaces, volumes, light-sources, films, expanses, degrees of solidity, solubility, temperature, elasticity, on color. Think of an object's capacity to emit, reflect, absorb, transmit, or scatter light; think of "the operation of light on a feather." Ask yourself, what is the color of a puddle? Is your blue sofa still blue when you stumble past it on your way to the kitchen for water in the middle of the night; is it still blue if you don't get up, and no one enters the room to see it? Fifteen days after we are born, we begin to discriminate between colors. For the rest of our lives, barring blunted or blinded sight, we find ourselves face-to-face with all these phenomena at once, and we call the whole shimmering mess "color." You might even say that it is the business of the eye to make colored forms out of what is essentially shimmering. This is how we "get around" in the world. Some might also call it the source of our suffering.

Is it still blue?

53. "We mainly suppose the experiential quality to be an intrinsic quality of the physical object"—this is the so-

called systematic illusion of color. Perhaps it is also that of love. But I am not willing to go there—not just yet. I believed in you.

54. Long before either wave or particle, some (Pythagoras, Euclid, Hipparchus) thought that our eyes emitted some kind of substance that illuminated, or "felt," what we saw. (Aristotle pointed out that this hypothesis runs into trouble at night, as objects become invisible despite the eyes' purported power.) Others, like Epicurus, proposed the inverse—that objects themselves project a kind of ray that reaches out toward the eye, as if they were looking at us (and surely some of them are). Plato split the difference, and postulated that a "visual fire" burns between our eyes and that which they behold. This still seems fair enough.

55. One image of the intellectual: a man who loses his eyesight not out of shame (Oedipus) but in order to think more clearly (Milton). I try to avoid generalities when it comes to the business of gender, but in all honesty I must admit that I simply cannot conceive of a version of female

intelligence that would advocate such a thing. An "abortion of the mind, this purity" (W. C. Williams).

56. There are, however, many stories of women—particularly saints—blinding themselves in order to maintain their chastity, to prove that they "only have eyes" for God or Christ. Consider, for example, the legend of Saint Lucy, patron saint of the blind, whose name means "clear, radiant, understandable." What seems clear enough: in 304 AD Lucy was tortured and put to death by the Roman emperor Diocletian, and thus martyred for her Christianity. What is unclear: why, exactly, she runs around Gothic and Renaissance paintings holding a golden dish with her blue eyes staring weirdly out from it. Some say her eyes were tortured out of her head in her martyrdom; some say she gouged them out herself after being sentenced by the pagan emperor to be defiled in a brothel. Even more unclear are the twinned legends of Saint Medana (of Ireland) and Saint Triduana (of Scotland), two Christian princesses who were pursued by undesirable pagan lovers—lovers who professed to be unable to live without their beloveds' beautiful blue eyes. To rid herself of the

unwanted attention, Medana supposedly plucked her eyes out and threw them at her suitor's feet; Triduana was slightly more inventive, and tore hers out with a thorn, then sent them to her suitor on a skewer.

57. In religious accounts, these women are announcing, via their amputations, their fidelity to God. But other accounts wonder whether they were in fact punishing themselves, as they knew that they had looked upon men with lust, and felt the need to employ extreme measures to avert any further temptation.

who is with lust

58. "Love is something so ugly that the human race would die out if lovers could see what they were doing" (Leonardo da Vinci).

blind for love.
blind is love.

59. There are those, however, who like to look. And we have not yet heard enough, if anything, about the female gaze. About the scorch of it, with the eyes staying in the head. "I love to gaze at a promising-looking cock," writes Catherine Millet in her beautiful sex memoir, before going on to describe how she also loves to look at the

"brownish crater" of her asshole and the "crimson valley" of her pussy, each opened wide—its color laid bare— for the fucking.

60. I like to look, too. "Saint Lucy, you did not hide your light under a basket," begins one Catholic prayer.

61. In his book *On Being Blue,* William Gass argues that what we readers really want is "the penetration of privacy": "We want to see under the skirt." But his penetration is eventually tiresome, even to himself: "What good is my peek at her pubic hair if I must also see the red lines made by her panties, the pimples on her rump, broken veins like the print of a lavender thumb, the stepped-on look of a day's-end muff? I've that at home." After asserting that the blue we want from life is in fact found only in fiction, he counsels the writer to "give up the blue things of this world in favor of the words which say them."

62. This is puritanism, not eros. For my part I have no interest in catching a glimpse of or offering you an unblemished ass or an airbrushed cunt. I am interested in having

three orifices stuffed full of thick, veiny cock in the most unforgiving of poses and light. I will not choose between the blue things of the world and the words that say them: you might as well be heating up the poker and readying your eyes for the altar. Your loss.

63. Generally speaking I do not hunt blue things down, nor do I pay for them. The blue things I treasure are gifts, or surprises in the landscape. The rocks I dug up this summer in the north country, for example, each one mysteriously painted round its belly with a bright blue band. The little square junk of navy blue dye you brought me long ago, when we barely knew each other, folded neatly into a paper wrapper.

64. It was around this time that I was planning to travel to many famously blue places: ancient indigo and woad production sites, the Chartres Cathedral, the Isle of Skye, the lapis mines of Afghanistan, the Scrovegni Chapel, Morocco, Crete. I made a map, I used colored pins, etc. But I had no money. So I applied for grant after grant, describing how exciting, how original, how *necessary* my

exploration of blue would be. In one application, written and sent late at night to a conservative Ivy League university, I described myself and my project as heathen, hedonistic, and horny. I never got any funding. My blues stayed local.

65. The instructions printed on the blue junk's wrapper: *Wrap Blue in cloth. Stir while squeezing the Blue in the last rinsing water. Dip articles separately for a short time; keep them moving.* I liked these instructions. I like blues that keep moving.

66. Yesterday I picked up a speck of blue I'd been eyeing for weeks on the ground outside my house, and found it to be a poison strip for termites. *Noli me tangere,* it said, as some blues do. I left it on the ground.

don't cling to me. "love"

"blue"

67. A male satin bowerbird would not have left it there. A male satin bowerbird would have tottered with it in his beak over to his bower, or his "trysting place," as some field guides put it, which he spends weeks adorning with blue objects in order to lure a female. Not only does the

26

bowerbird collect and arrange blue objects—bus tickets, cicada wings, blue flowers, bottle caps, blue feathers plucked off smaller blue birds that he kills, if he must, to get their plumage—but he also paints his bower with juices from blue fruits, using the frayed end of a twig as a paintbrush. He builds competitively, stealing treasures from other birds, sometimes trashing their bowers entirely.

68. After building his bower, the satin bowerbird makes a stage nearby out of shiny yellow grass, upon which he will sing and dance for passing females. Experienced builders and performers can attract up to thirty-three females to fuck per season if they put on a good enough show, have built up enough good blue in their bower, and have the contrast with the yellow straw down right. Less experienced builders sometimes don't attract any females at all. Each female mates only once. She incubates the eggs alone. *don't cling to him.*

69. When I see photos of these blue bowers, I feel so much desire that I wonder if I might have been born into the wrong species.

" statements that express ↑ opinion."

70. Am I trying, with these "propositions," to build some kind of bower? —But surely this would be a mistake. For starters, *words do not* look like *the things they designate* (Maurice Merleau-Ponty).

71. I have been trying, for some time now, to find dignity in my loneliness. I have been finding this hard to do.

loneliness v.s. solitude.

72. It is easier, of course, to find dignity in one's solitude. Loneliness is solitude with a problem. Can blue solve the problem, or can it at least keep me company within it? —No, not exactly. It cannot love me that way; it has no arms. But sometimes I do feel its presence to be a sort of wink—*Here you are again,* it says, *and so am I.*

73. In his *Opticks,* Newton periodically refers to an invaluable "assistant" who helps him refract the shaft of sunlight streaming in through the aperture Newton had drilled into the wall of his "dark chamber"—an assistant to Newton's discovery, or revelation, of the spectrum. Over time, however, many have questioned whether this assistant ever really existed. Many now believe him to be, essentially, a "rhetorical fiction."

74. Who, nowadays, watches the light stream through the walls of her "dark chamber" with the company of a phantasmagoric assistant, or smashes at her eyes to reproduce lost color sensations, or stays up all night watching colored shadows drift across the walls? At times I have done all of these things, but not in service of science, nor of philosophy, not even of poetry.

75. Mostly I have felt myself becoming a servant of sadness. I am still looking for the beauty in that.

76. At one point in history, to approximate the color of ultramarine, which comes from lapis, which for quite some time was available in only one mine, in what we now call Afghanistan—*Sar-e-Sang, the Place of the Stone*—and had to be journeyed out via hundreds of miles of treacherous trade roads, Westerners would churn up cheaper pigments with blood and copper. Generally speaking we don't do this anymore. We don't store our oils in the bladders of pigs. We go to the store. If we want to know what a phosphene is, we don't mash our fists into our eyes. We Google the word. If you're depressed, you take a pill. Some of these pills are bright blue. If you're lonely,

不用 experiential
不用 live through.

29

there's a guy on Craigslist two blocks away who says he has an hour to kill and a dick longer than a donkey's. He has posted a photograph to prove it.

77. "Why should I feel lonely? is not our planet in the Milky Way?" (Thoreau).

78. Once I traveled to the Tate in London to see the blue paintings of Yves Klein, who invented and patented his own shade of ultramarine, International Klein Blue (IKB), then painted canvases and objects with it throughout a period of his life he dubbed "l'epoque bleue." Standing in front of these blue paintings, or propositions, at the Tate, feeling their blue radiate out so hotly that it seemed to be touching, perhaps even hurting, my eyeballs, I wrote but one phrase in my notebook: *too much.* I had come all this way, and I could barely look. Perhaps I had inadvertently brushed up against the Buddhist axiom, that enlightenment is the ultimate disappointment. "From the mountain you see the mountain," wrote Emerson.

79. For just because one loves blue does not mean that one wants to spend one's life in a world made of it. "Life is a

train of moods like a string of beads, and as we pass through them they prove to be many-colored lenses which paint the world their own hue, and each shows only what lies in its focus," wrote Emerson. To find one-self trapped in any one bead, no matter what its hue, can be deadly.

80. What I have heard: when the mines of Sar-e-Sang run dry (locals say the repressive rule of the Taliban, who, in 2000, blew up the two giant statues of Buddha at the mines' entrance—Buddhas whose blue auras were the oldest-known application of lapis on earth—caused a particularly long dry spell; God only knows what the American bombing has done since), the miners use dy-namite to bleed a vein, in hopes of starting a "blue rush."

blue
↓
love

81. What I know: when I met you, a blue rush began. I want you to know, I no longer hold you responsible.

82. I have made efforts, however fitful, to live within other beads. During one particularly despondent New York City winter, I bought a huge can of bright yellow paint at the hardware store on Allen Street, imagining that I might

31

buoy my soul with its cheer. When I got home and pried off the lid I realized they'd given me the wrong color, or maybe it was the right one, but at home it looked garish —like "death warmed over," as they say. It was a terrible yellow, a yellow of utter rage. Later I learned that nearly all cultures have considered yellow in isolation one of, if not *the* least attractive of all colors. I painted everything with it.

83. I tried to go with the theme: I bought a yellow journal. On its cover sheet I wrote a slogan of penetration: *Do not tell lies and do not do what you hate, for all things are manifest in the sight of heaven.*

Ironic

84. I hated that time and I hated that apartment and soon after I painted everything yellow I moved out. I looked at dozens of apartments and when I entered the hallway of the one I moved into next I knew I could live there because it was cheap and the hallway was baby blue. My friends all told me it smelled as bad there as it did in the last one but I found a heads-up penny on the threshold and anyway I don't live there anymore.

85. One afternoon in 2006, at a bookstore in Los Angeles. I pick up a book called *The Deepest Blue.* Having expected a chromatic treatise, I am embarrassed when I see the subtitle: *How Women Face and Overcome Depression.* I quickly return it to its shelf. Eight months later, I order the book online.

86. The implication of the title is that men get blue, but women get *the deepest blue.* Another form of aggrandizement, to be sure—one which brings to mind a night I spent in an emergency room in Brooklyn years ago—some mystery ailment, a burning in my lower left side—a woman wailing in the waiting room about having gas from fried chicken, though she looked riddled with crack and sadness, not gas from fried chicken—a young doctor inside asked me to rate my pain on a scale of 1 to 10—I was flummoxed, I felt as though I shouldn't be there at all—I said "6"—he said to the nurse, Write down "8," since women always underestimate their pain. Men always say "11," he said. I didn't believe him, but I supposed he might know.

87. "Great suffering, joy, exertion, is not for [woman]; her life should flow by more quietly, trivially, gently than the man's without being essentially happier or unhappier," wrote Schopenhauer. What women, one would like to ask, did he know? At any rate, *would that it were so.*

88. Like many self-help books, *The Deepest Blue* is full of horrifyingly simplistic language and some admittedly good advice. Somehow the women in the book all learn to say: *That's my depression talking. It's not "me."*

but my depression is me. or I'm serving the depression

89. As if we could scrape the color off the iris and still see.

90. Last night I wept in a way I haven't wept for some time. I wept until I aged myself. I watched it happen in the mirror. I watched the lines arrive around my eyes like en-graved sunbursts; it was like watching flowers open in time-lapse on a windowsill. The tears not only aged my face, they also changed its texture, turned the skin of my cheeks into putty. I recognized this as a rite of decadence, but I did not know how to stop it.

91. *Blue-eye,* archaic: "a blueness or dark circle around the eye, from weeping or other cause."

92. Eventually I confess to a friend some details about my weeping—its intensity, its frequency. She says (kindly) that she thinks we sometimes weep in front of a mirror not to inflame self-pity, but because we want to feel witnessed in our despair. (*Can a reflection be a witness? Can one pass oneself the sponge wet with vinegar from a reed?*)

93. "At first glance, it seems strange to think that an innocuous, inborn behavior such as crying could be dysfunctional or symptomatic," writes one clinical psychologist. But, this psychologist insists, we must face the fact that some crying is simply "maladaptive, dysfunctional, or immature."

94. —Well then, it is as you please. This is the dysfunction talking. This is the disease talking. This is how much I miss you talking. This is the deepest blue, talking, talking, always talking to you.

95. But please don't write again to tell me how you have woken up weeping. I already know how you are in love with your weeping.

96. For a prince of blue is a prince of blue because he keeps "a pet sorrow, a blue-devil familiar, that goes with him everywhere" (Lowell, 1870). This is how a prince of blue becomes a pain devil.

thread.

97. And now, I think, we can say: a glass bead may flush the world with color, but it alone makes no necklace. I wanted the necklace.

98. Vincent van Gogh, whose depression, some say, was likely related to temporal lobe epilepsy, famously saw and painted the world in almost unbearably vivid colors. After his nearly unsuccessful attempt to take his life by shooting himself in the gut, when asked why he should not be saved, he famously replied, "The sadness will last forever." I imagine he was right.

99. After a few months in the hospital, my injured friend is visited by a fellow quadriparalytic as part of an out-

"normal"

reach program. From her bed she asks him, *If I remain paralyzed, how long will it take for my injury to feel like a normal part of my life?* At least five years, he told her. As of next month, she will be at three.

100. It often happens that we count our days, as if the act of measurement made us some kind of promise. But really this is like hoisting a harness onto an invisible horse. "There is simply no way that a year from now you're going to feel the way you feel today," a different therapist said to me last year at this time. But though I have learned to act as if I feel differently, the truth is that my feelings haven't really changed.

101. "The years of the second war, and the decades after, were a blinding, bad time for me, about which I could not say a thing even if I wanted to," says a character in W. G. Sebald's *The Emigrants.* After reading this I polled several friends to see how much time they would grant between "a blinding, bad time" and a life that has simply become a depressive waste; the consensus was around seven years. This bespeaks the generosity of my friends —I imagine that most Americans would give themselves

about a year, maybe two, before they castigated themselves into some form of yanking up the bootstraps. On
September 21, 2001, for example, George Bush II told the
country that the time for grief had passed, and the time
for resolute action had taken its place.

102. After my friend's accident I take care of her. It is always taking care, but it is difficult, because at times to take
care of her is also to cause her pain. For two years, to get
her in and out of her wheelchair, we have to perform a
complicated maneuver called "the transfer." "The transfer" often sends her legs into excruciating spasms, during
which time all I can do is press down on them and say, *I'm
sorry, I'm so sorry,* until the shaking stops. She has diffuse nerve pain along the surface of her skin which no
doctor understands, pain she says makes her skin feel like
crinkly, burning Saran Wrap. We look at her skin together
as she describes this pain.

103. When the pain is bad it drains her color. When it
breaks through the drugs, of which there are many, she
says it feels like a scrim goes up between her and the rest

of the world. In my mind's eye, I imagine it as an invisible jacket of burn hovering between us.

104. I do not feel my friend's pain, but when I unintentionally cause her pain I wince as if I hurt somewhere, and I do. Often in exhaustion I lay my head down on her lap in her wheelchair and tell her how much I love her, that I'm so sorry she is in so much pain, pain I can witness and imagine but that I do not know. She says, if anyone knows this pain besides me, it is you (and J, her lover). This is generous, for to be close to her pain has always felt like a privilege to me, even though pain could be defined as that which we typically aim to avoid. Perhaps this is because she remains so generous *within* hers, and because she has never held any hierarchy of grief, either before her accident or after, which seems to me nothing less than a form of enlightenment.

105. There are no instruments for measuring color; there are no "color thermometers." How could there be, as "color knowledge" always remains contingent upon an individual perceiver? This didn't stop a certain Horace

Bénédict de Saussure, however, from inventing, in 1789, a device he called the "cyanometer," with which he hoped to measure the blue of the sky.

106. When I first heard of the cyanometer, I imagined a complicated machine with dials, cranks, and knobs. But what de Saussure actually "invented" was a cardboard chart with 53 cut-out squares sitting alongside 53 numbered swatches, or "nuances," as he called them, of blue: you simply hold the sheet up to the sky and match its color, to the best of your ability, to a swatch. As in *Humboldt's Travels* (Ross, 1852): "We beheld with admiration the azure colour of the sky. Its intensity at the zenith appeared to correspond to 41° of the cyanometer." This latter sentence brings me great pleasure, but really it takes us no further—either into knowledge, or into beauty.

107. Many people do not think the writing of Gertrude Stein "means" anything. Perhaps it does not. But when my students complain that they want to throw *Tender Buttons* across the room, I try to explain to them that in it Stein is dealing with a matter of pressing concern. *Stein*

is worried about hurt colors, I tell them. "A spectacle and nothing strange a single hurt color and an arrangement in a system to pointing," I read aloud, scanning the room for a face that also shows signs of being worried about hurt colors. "Enthusiastically hurting a clouded yellow bud and saucer." "A cool red rose and a pink cut pink." As if color could be further revealed by *slitting.*

108. Think, for example, of Leonard Cohen's "famous blue raincoat," whose principal attribute is that it is "torn at the shoulder." Perhaps it is even the tear that makes it famous. The song features Cohen at his most lugubrious and opaque, which is saying a lot, but I have always loved its final line—"Sincerely, L. Cohen"—as it makes me feel less alone in composing almost everything I write as a letter. I would even go so far as to say that I do not know how to compose otherwise, which makes writing in a prism of solitude, as I am here, a somewhat novel and painful experiment. "When our companion fails us we transfer our love instantaneously to a worthy object," wrote Thoreau during his bitter falling-out with Emerson, unwittingly offering a cogent explanation of how and why so many

songwriters have personified blue as the one friend they can count on. It "loves me when I'm lonely / And thinks of me first," sings Lucinda Williams. But really this is very strange—as if blue not only had a heart, but also a *mind*.

109. Over time my injured friend's feet have become blue and smooth from disuse. Their blue is the blue of skim milk, their smoothness that of a baby's. I think they look and feel very strange and beautiful. She does not agree. How could she—this is her body; its transformations, her grief. Often we examine parts of her body together, as if their paralysis had rendered them objects of inquiry independent of us both. But they are still hers. No matter what happens to our bodies in our lifetimes, no matter if they become like "pebbles in water," they remain ours; us, theirs.

110. In *Tender Buttons,* Stein seems particularly worried about color and pain that seem to come from nowhere, for no reason. "Why is there a single piece of any color . . . Why is there so much useless suffering." About blue itself, Stein offers but this koan: "Every bit of blue is precocious."

111. Goethe also worries about colors and pain, though his reports sound more like installments from the battlefield: "Every decided colour does a certain violence to the eye, and forces the organ to opposition." Instantly I recognize this phenomenon to be true from my years of working in a bright orange restaurant. I worked in this restaurant for ten-hour shifts, from 4 p.m. to 2 a.m., sometimes later. The restaurant was incredibly orange. In fact everyone in town called it "the orange restaurant." Yet every time I came home from work and passed out in my smoke-drenched clothes, my feet propped up on the wall, the dining room reappeared in my dreams as pale blue. For quite some time I thought this was luck, or wish fulfillment—naturally my dreams would convert everything to blue, because of my love for the color. But now I realize that it was more likely the result of spending ten hours or more staring at saturated orange, blue's spectral opposite. This is a simple story, but it spooks me, insofar as it reminds me that the eye is simply a recorder, with or without our will. Perhaps the same could be said of the heart. But whether there is a *violence* at work here remains undecided.

112. At times I have heard it said that we don't dream in color. But surely this is a mistake. Not only can we dream in color, but more importantly: how could anyone else know if we do or do not? At times I have been tempted to think that we dream more colorfully now because of the cinema. (To know what dreams were like before the cinema!) But then I think of "The Dream of the Rood," one of the first documents in Old English, from around the eighth century, which flickers with color (and with pleasure, and with pain): "Behold I shall tell of a most marvelous dream . . . It seemed to me that I saw a tree, more wonderful than any other, spring high aloft, bathed in light, brightest of wood. All that beacon was covered in gold . . . Wonderful was the triumphant tree, and I stained with sin, wounded with wrongdoing . . . I was sadly troubled, afraid of that fair sight. I saw that beacon, changeable, alter in clothes and color: now it was wet with moisture, drenched with blood's flowing, now adorned with treasure." The question of whether gold counts as a color may here arise, but I am not equipped to tackle it. I will relay only this: "What is on the other side of gold is the

same as what is on this side" (John Berger); I'm tempted to think this disqualifies it. The red of the dreamer's wrongdoing, however, appears nonnegotiable.

113. In his unfinished novel *Heinrich von Ofterdingen,* Novalis tells the story of a medieval troubadour who sees a little blue flower—perhaps a bluet—in a dream. Afterward he longs to see the blue flower in "real life." "I can't get rid of the idea," he says. "It haunts me." (Mallarmé, too: "*Je suis hanté. L'Azur! l'Azur! l'Azur! l'Azur!*") Heinrich knows his obsession is a little singular: "For who would be so concerned about a flower in this world? And I've never heard of anyone being in love with a flower." Nonetheless, he devotes his life to searching for it: thus begins the adventure, the high romance, the romance of seeking.

114. But now think of the Dutch expression: "*Dat zijn maar blauwe bloempjes*"—"Those are nothing but blue flowers." In which case "blue flowers" means a pack of bald-faced lies.

115. In which case seeking itself is a spiritual error.

116. One of the last times you came to see me, you were wearing a pale blue button-down shirt, short-sleeved. *I wore this for you,* you said. We fucked for six hours straight that afternoon, which does not seem precisely possible but that is what the clock said. We killed the time. You were on your way to a seaside town, a town of much blue, where you would be spending a week with the other woman you were in love with, the woman you are with now. *I'm in love with you both in completely different ways,* you said. It seemed unwise to contemplate this statement any further.

117. "How clearly I have seen my condition, yet how childishly I have acted," says Goethe's sorrowful young Werther. "How clearly I still see it, and yet show no sign of improvement."

118. Not long after that afternoon I came across a photo-graph of you with this woman. You were wearing the shirt. I went over to the house of my injured friend and

told her the story as I moved her legs in and out of the inflatable, thigh-high boots she wears to compress her legs while lying down so as to inhibit the formation of blood clots. *How ghastly,* she said.

119. My friend was a genius before her accident, and she remains a genius now. The difference is that these days it is nearly impossible to discount her pronouncements. Something about her condition has bestowed upon her the quality of an oracle, perhaps because now she generally stays in one place, and one must go unto her. *Eventually you will have to give up this love,* she told me one night while I made us dinner. *It has a morbid heart.*

120. In the end, climactically rebuffed, young Werther shoots himself in the head while wearing a blue coat—a coat which is a replica of the one he was wearing the night he first danced with his beloved. It then takes him all night to die a bloody death that inspired a rash of copycat, blue-coated suicides all over Germany and beyond. Note that here, as elsewhere, *seeing clearly* seems to take Werther, and us, no further.

121. "Clearness is so eminently one of the characteristics of truth, that often it even passes for truth itself," wrote Joseph Joubert, the French "man of letters" who recorded countless such fragments in notebooks for forty years in preparation for a monumental work of philosophy that he never wrote. I know all about this passing for truth. At times I think it quite possible that it lies, as if a sleight of hand, at the heart of all my writing.

122. "Truth. To surround it with figures and colors, so that it can be seen," wrote Joubert, calmly professing a heresy.

123. Whenever I speak of faith, I am not speaking of faith in God. Likewise, when I speak of doubt, I am not talking about doubting God's existence, or the truth of any gospel. Such terms have never meant very much to me. To contemplate them reminds me of playing Pin the Tail on the Donkey: you get spun around until you wander off, disoriented and blindfolded, walking gingerly with a hand stretched out in front of you, until you either run into a wall (laughter), or a friend gently pushes you back toward the game.

124. On this account I am prepared to call myself a "spiritual cripple," as a Japanese critic once said of Sei Shōnagon, author of the famous *Makura no Sōshi,* or "Notes of the Pillow." This critic was appalled by Shōnagon's obsession with trivia, aesthetics, and gossip, her hostility toward men, and by her unbridled, unrepentantly malicious comments about others, especially those of lower classes. A few of the pillow book's many lists: "Things that give a pathetic impression," "Things without merit," "People who seem to suffer."

125. Of course, you could also just take off the blindfold and say, *I think this game is stupid, and I'm not playing it anymore.* And it must also be admitted that hitting the wall or wandering off in the wrong direction or tearing off the blindfold is as much a part of the game as is pinning the tail on the donkey.

126. One of Shōnagon's first entries describes her delight in the Festival of Blue Horses, a day on which twenty-one glorious gray-blue horses from the Imperial stables are paraded in front of the Emperor. Reading her account, I feel at once the need to die and be reborn one thousand

years ago, so as to see this parade for myself. But here we are in great danger—the danger of being jealous of the blues of others, or of blues of times past. For while one may repeatedly insist that all one wants is to be satisfied and happy, the truth is that one can often find oneself clinging to samsara with a vengeance. This is especially so when one starts to get the sense—however dim—that there might in fact be a way to unloose oneself from the wheel. "Nostalgia for samsara," some Buddhists call this affliction, the talons of which seem to grow but sharper as soon as one begins to understand the importance of escaping them.

127. Ask yourself: what is the color of a jacaranda tree in bloom? You once described it to me as "a type of blue." I did not know then if I agreed, for I had not yet seen the tree.

128. When you first told me about the jacarandas I felt hopeful. Then, the first time I saw them myself, I felt despair. The next season, I felt despair again. And so we arrive at one instance, and then another, upon which blue

delivered a measure of despair. But truth be told: I saw them as purple.

129. I don't know how the jacarandas will make me feel next year. I don't know if I will be alive to see them, or if I will be here to see them, or if I will ever be able to see them as blue, even as a type of blue.

130. We cannot read the darkness. We cannot read it. It is a form of madness, albeit a common one, that we try.

131. "I just don't feel like you're trying hard *enough,*" one friend says to me. How can I tell her that *not trying* has become the whole point, the whole plan?

132. That is to say: I have been trying to go limp in the face of my heartache, as another friend says he does in the face of his anxiety. *Think of it as an act of civil disobedience,* he says. *Let the police peel you up.*

133. I have been trying to place myself in a land of great sunshine, and abandon my will therewith.

134. It calms me to think of blue as the color of death. I have long imagined death's approach as the swell of a wave—a towering wall of blue. *You will drown,* the world tells me, has always told me. *You will descend into a blue underworld, blue with hungry ghosts, Krishna blue, the blue faces of the ones you loved. They all drowned, too.* To take a breath of water: does the thought panic or excite you? If you are in love with red then you slit or shoot. If you are in love with blue you fill your pouch with stones good for sucking and head down to the river. Any river will do.

135. Of course one can have "the blues" and stay alive, at least for a time. "Productive," even (the perennial consolation!). See, for example, "Lady Sings the Blues": "She's got them bad / She feels so sad / Wants the world to know / Just what her blues is all about." Nonetheless, as Billie Holiday knew, it remains the case that to see blue in deeper and deeper saturation is eventually to move toward darkness.

136. "Drinking when you are depressed is like throwing kerosene on a fire," I read in another self-help book at the

bookstore. *What depression ever felt like a fire?* I think, shoving the book back on the shelf.

137. It is unclear what Holiday means, exactly, when she sings, "But now the world will know / She's never gonna sing 'em no more / No more." What is unclear: whether she is moving on, shutting up, or going to die. Also unclear: the source of her *triumphance*.

138. But perhaps there is no real mystery here at all. "Life is usually stronger than people's love for it" (Adam Phillips): *this* is what Holiday's voice makes audible. To hear it is to understand why suicide is both so easy and so difficult: to commit it one has to stamp out this native triumphance, either by training oneself, over time, to dehabilitate or disbelieve it (drugs help here), or by force of *ambush*.

139. "Memory is blue in the head? Heads are easily taken off" (Lorine Niedecker).

140. How to take it off: I could drink every single drop of alcohol in my house, which includes the rest of this beer

and a bottle of Maker's Mark. I could let myself be fucked mercilessly by many strangers at once, as in my first sexual fantasy: I am sent halfway across the world in a cardboard box with a lot of postage on it. The journey is long and rough and invariably involves much jostling by camels. When I arrive, a tribe of men opens the box under a hot desert sun, and out spills my small body. They are all eager to touch it.

141. I have also imagined my life ending, or simply evaporating, by being subsumed into a tribe of blue people. I dreamed of these blue people as a child, long before I knew that such people actually existed. Now I know that they do, in the eastern and central Sahara desert, and that they are called *Tuareg*, which means "abandoned by God." I also know that many Westerners—including several Western women—have shared in this fantasy. I know that it bears all the marks of an unforgivable exoticism. But the fact remains that I have been dreaming about these blue people for a long time—long before I knew the story of Isabelle Eberhardt, for example, who left Switzerland for North Africa as a young child, cross-dressed

as a man her entire life, and eventually got lost among a mystical sect in the desert called the Qadriya before dying in a flash flood in Ain Sefra, her body "carried downstream along with scores of other corpses" and eventually crushed by a beam. In the rubble of this flood was found a partial manuscript of her book, *The Oblivion Seekers,* a collection one critic has described as "one of the strangest human documents that a woman has given to the world." Its first story begins: "Long and white, the road twists like a snake toward the far-off blue places, toward the bright edges of the earth."

142. To seek these far-off blue places is, for Eberhardt, to seek oblivion. And to seek oblivion is, for Eberhardt, to be a smoker of kif. "An open wound," she describes a den of kif.

143. Near the end of her relatively brief life (she died at forty-four), many were calling Holiday's voice "ravaged"—by dope, by booze, by abuse, by sorrow. Though no junkie, Joni Mitchell, too, now consistently bears the "ravaged" epithet. "If the health warning isn't enough

to put you off cigarettes, the nicotine-ravaged vocals of the once angelic, now gasping Joni Mitchell should," one reviewer recently wrote. "Mitchell's voice is a husky shadow of its former feather-light glory, mirroring how her joyful, playful attitude has dwindled to bitter dissatisfaction."

144. Then again, perhaps it does feel like a fire—the blue core of it, not the theatrical orange crackling. I have spent a lot of time staring at this core in my own "dark chamber," and I can testify that it provides an excellent example of how blue gives way to darkness—and then how, without warning, the darkness grows up into a cone of light.

145. In German, to be blue—*blau sein*—means to be drunk. *Delirium tremens* used to be called the "blue devils," as in "my bitter hours of blue-devilism" (Burns, 1787). In England "the blue hour" is happy hour at the pub. Joan Mitchell—abstract painter of the first order, American expatriate living on Monet's property in France, dedicated chromophile and drunk, possessor of

a famously nasty tongue, and creator of arguably my favorite painting of all time, *Les Bluets,* which she painted in 1973, the year of my birth—found the green of spring incredibly irritating. She thought it was bad for her work. She would have preferred to live perpetually in "l'heure de bleu." Her dear friend Frank O'Hara understood. *Ah daddy, I wanna stay drunk many days,* he wrote, and did.

146. "When a woman drinks it's as if an animal were drinking, or a child," Marguerite Duras once wrote. "It's a slur on the divine in our nature." In *Crack Wars,* Avital Ronell refers to Duras's works as "alchoholizations"—as *saturated,* so to speak, with the substance. Could one imagine a book similarly saturated, but with color? How could one tell the difference? And if "saturation" means that one simply could not absorb or contain one single drop more, why does "saturation" not bring with it a connotation of satisfaction, either in concept, or in experience?

147. "Rather than your face as a young woman, I prefer your face as it is now. Ravaged," a man tells the narrator in

the opening lines of Duras's *The Lover*. For many years, I took these to be the words of a wise man.

148. The Tuareg wear flowing robes so bright and rich with blue that over time the dye has seeped into their skin, literally blueing it. They are desert nomads who were famously unwilling to be converted to Islam: thus their name. Some American Christians have been bothered by this idea of a blue people abandoned by God living in the Sahara, herding camels, traveling by night, and navigating by the stars. In Virginia, in 2002, for example, a group of Southern Baptists organized a day of prayer exclusively for the Tuareg, "so that they will know God loves them."

149. It should be noted that the Tuareg do not call themselves Tuareg. Nor do they call themselves the blue people. They call themselves *Imohag*, which means "free men."

150. For Plato, color was as dangerous a narcotic as poetry. He wanted both out of the republic. He called painters

"mixers and grinders of multi-colored drugs," and color itself a form of *pharmakon*. The religious zealots of the Reformation felt similarly: they smashed the stained-glass windows of churches, thinking them idolatrous, degenerate. For distinct reasons, which had to do with the fight to keep the cheap, slave-labor crop of indigo out of a Western market long dominated by woad, the blue-dye-producing plant native to Europe, indigo blue was called "the devil's dye." And before blue became a "holy" color—which had to do with the advent of ultramarine in the twelfth century, and its subsequent use in stained glass and religious paintings—it often symbolized the Antichrist.

151. Ultramarine is not, of course, holy in and of itself. (What is?) It had to be *made* holy, by the wicked logic that renders the expensive sacred. So first it had to be made expensive. From the start, however, its preciousness stemmed from a sort of misunderstanding: ancient peoples thought the shining veins in lapis lazuli were gold, when really they are iron pyrite: "fool's gold."

152. Holiness and evilness aside, no one could rightly call blue a *festive* color. You don't go looking for a party in a color that hospitals have used to calm crying infants or sedate the emotionally disturbed. Ancient Egyptians wrapped their mummies in blue cloth; ancient Celtic warriors dyed their bodies with woad before heading off to battle; the Aztecs smeared the chests of their sacrificial victims with blue paint before scooping their hearts out on the altar; the story of indigo is, at least in part, the story of slavery, riots, and misery. Blue does, however, always have a place at the *carnival*.

153. I've read that children pretty much prefer red hands-down over all other colors; the shift into liking cooler tones—such as blue—happens as they grow older. Nowadays half the adults in the Western world say that blue is their favorite color. In their international survey of the "Most Wanted Painting," the Russian émigré team Vitaly Komar and Alex Melamid discovered that country after country—from China to Finland to Germany to the United States to Russia to Kenya to Turkey—most wanted a blue landscape, with slight variances (a ballerina here, a moose there, and so on). The only exception

was Holland, which, for inscrutable reasons, wanted a murky, rainbow-hued abstraction.

154. It is tempting to derive some kind of maturity narrative here: eventually we sober up and grow out of our rash love of intensity (i.e. red); eventually we learn to love more subtle things with more subtlety, etc. etc. But my love for blue has never felt to me like a maturing, or a refinement, or a *settling*. For the fact is that one can maintain a chromophilic recklessness well into adulthood. Joan Mitchell, for one, customarily chose her pigments for their intensity rather than their durability—a choice that, as many painters know, can in time bring one's paintings into a sorry state of decay. (Is writing spared this phenomenon?)

155. It does not really bother me that half the adults in the Western world also love blue, or that every dozen years or so someone feels compelled to write a book about it. I feel confident enough of the specificity and strength of my relation to it to share. Besides, it must be admitted that if blue is anything on this earth, it is *abundant*.

156. "Why is the sky blue?" —A fair enough question, and one I have learned the answer to several times. Yet every time I try to explain it to someone or remember it to myself, it eludes me. Now I like to remember the question alone, as it reminds me that my mind is essentially a sieve, that I am mortal.

157. The part I do remember: that the blue of the sky depends on the darkness of empty space behind it. As one optics journal puts it, "The color of any planetary atmosphere viewed against the black of space and illuminated by a sunlike star will also be blue." In which case blue is something of an ecstatic accident produced by void and fire.

158. God is truth; truth is light; God is light; etc.: the chain of syllogisms goes on and on. See John 1:5: "And the light shineth in darkness; and the darkness comprehended it not." (As if darkness, too, had a mind.)

159. A good many have figured God as light, but a good many have also figured him as darkness. Dionysius the Areopagite, a Syrian monk whose work and identity are

themselves shrouded in obscurity, would seem to be one of the first serious Christian advocates of the idea of a "Divine Darkness." The idea is a complicated one, as the burden falls to us to differentiate this Divine Darkness from other kinds of darknesses—that of a "dark night of the soul," the darkness of sin, and so on. "We pray that we may come unto this Darkness which is beyond light, and, without seeing and without knowing, to see and to know that which is above vision and knowledge through the realization that by not-seeing and unknowing we attain to true vision and knowledge," Dionysius wrote, as if clarifying the matter.

160. Equally complicated: the idea of *agnosia*, or *unknowing*, which is what one ideally finds, or undergoes, or achieves, within this Divine Darkness. Again: this *agnosia* is not a form of ignorance, but rather a kind of *undoing*. (As if one knew once, then forgot? But what did one know?)

161. Philosopher Bertrand Russell was a fan of Wittgenstein's early work in logic, but he complained that the later Wittgenstein "seems to have grown tired of serious

thinking and to have invented a doctrine which would make such an activity unnecessary." I am not sure if I agree, but I note the temptation. So, I think, did Wittgenstein. "Explanations come to an end somewhere," he wrote.

162. According to Dionysius, the Divine Darkness appears dark only because it is so dazzlingly bright—a paradox I have attempted to understand by looking directly at the sun and noticing the dark spot that flowers at its center. But as compelling as this paradox, or this experiment, may be, I am not as interested in it as I am in the fact that in Christian iconography, this "dazzling darkness" appears with startling regularity as blue.

163. Why blue? There is no basis for it in the Scriptures. In the Gospel accounts of the Transfiguration—ground zero, as it were, for the onset of this "bright cloud" of *agnosia*—the cloud is shadow, Jesus's raiment a "glistering" white. Yet for the past two thousand years, in mosaic after mosaic, painting after painting, Jesus stands transfigured before his witnesses in the mouth of a glowing

blue *mandorla*—a blue almond, or *vesica piscus,* the shape that, in pagan times, unabashedly symbolized Venus and the vulva.

164. I do not know the reason for this blue pussy, meant to convey both divine bewilderment and revelation. But I do feel that its color is right. For blue has no mind. It is not wise, nor does it promise any wisdom. It is beautiful, and despite what the poets and philosophers and theologians have said, I think beauty neither obscures truth nor reveals it. Likewise, it leads neither toward justice nor away from it. It is *pharmakon.* It *radiates.*

165. Two of the blue correspondents—two filmmakers— have just reported from the field to say that they have undertaken a rescue project, a rescue of soon-to-be-lost blues. As the digital age steamrolls ahead, most films are being rapidly digitized. And as the digitization process privileges green over both red and blue, the correspondents have decided to collect the blues that "fall out" of film during the transfer. They say they have to act fast. I do not know what they will do with their collection, or

what form, exactly, "fallen-out" blues will take. I imagine it will be a sort of muddle.

166. The 1939 film *The Women* was shot entirely in black and white, with the exception of one Technicolor sequence—a fashion show—which was literally detachable from the rest of the film. This colored reel had no bearing on the plot whatsoever, so the projectionist could choose to insert it as part of the movie or ignore it altogether. Could one imagine a book that functioned similarly, albeit in reverse—a kind of optional, black-and-white appendage to a larger body of blue (e.g., "the blue planet")?

167. I don't go to the movies anymore. Please don't try to convince me. When something ceases to bring you pleasure, you cannot *talk* the pleasure back into it. "My removal arose not out of a conscious decision, but was simply a natural fading away from film," writes artist Mike Kelley. "We have become filmic language, and when we look at the screen all we see is ourselves. So what is there to fall into or be consumed by? When looking at something that purports to be you, all you can do is comment

on whether you feel it is a good resemblance or not. Is it a flattering portrait? This is a conscious, clearly ego-directed, activity." I find myself in agreement with him on all counts. Perhaps this is why I have turned my gaze so insistently to blue: it does not purport to be me, or anyone else for that matter. "I think both the theater and we ourselves have had enough of psychology" (Artaud).

168. Cézanne, too, had had enough of psychology. He attended, instead, to color. "If I paint all the little blues and all the little browns, I capture and convey his glance," he said of painting a man's face. This may be but a colorized restatement of Wittgenstein's remark, "if only you do not try to utter what is unutterable then *nothing* gets lost. But the unutterable will be– unutterably—*contained* in what has been uttered!" Perhaps this is why I take the blues of Cézanne so seriously.

169. Despite his falling away from film, Kelley remains charmed by Joseph Cornell's 1936 film *Rose Hobart,* a collage of found footage of a jungle B-movie called *East of Borneo.* Using scissors and tape, Cornell cut *East of*

Borneo down from 77 minutes to 19½, focusing fairly exclusively on shots of Rose Hobart, the movie's spunky female lead. Cornell's instructions for the film state that it should be screened with a soundtrack of Latin dance music, and that it should be projected through a deep blue filter, so as to bathe Rose in the color he so loved.

170. Cornell even coined a word to describe the sensation he hoped to produce by blue-tinting his work: "Blueaille." I have no idea how he pronounced it, which is fine by me—this way it can be "bluet" (like the flower), "blueail" (like an affliction), or "blue-aye" (like Versailles, or blue-eye). Unlike Yves Klein, however, Cornell had no urge to patent his invention (which is just as well, as you can't yet patent a sensation, thank God). Cornell was a gatherer, not an owner. He was also a builder of bowers, which he called "habitats," as befits someone who adored birds. "Day / and I gathered fragments of blue dense," he wrote in an undated scribble.

171. When one begins to gather "fragments of blue dense," one might think one is paying tribute to the blue

wholes from which they came. But a bouquet is no homage to the bush. Over the years I have amassed countless blue stones, blue shards of glass, blue marbles, trampled blue photographs peeled off sidewalks, pieces of blue rubble from broken buildings, and though I can't remember where most of them came from, I love them nonetheless.

172. To stumble upon discarded canisters of a bad Hollywood movie, to cut the reels up in an effort to isolate the thing you love to gaze upon most, to project the resulting patchwork through the lens of your favorite color, alongside a bustling "tropical" soundtrack: this seems to me, right now, the perfect film. But there is one other important candidate: Warhol's *Blue Movie,* otherwise known as *Fuck.* "I'd always wanted to do a movie that was pure fucking, nothing else," Warhol said, and in October of 1968, he did.

173. In July of 1969, *Blue Movie* was seized by the police for obscenity, and was then not screened publicly for years. When the obscenity issue faded away, one of its

fuckers, Viva, suppressed the film on the grounds that she'd never signed a release for it. By 2005, Viva had apparently changed her mind, and she appeared with the film at several festivals. But as I saw neither it nor her, it would be unjust to say any more on the subject.

174. Mallarmé might have felt otherwise. For Mallarmé, the perfect book was one whose pages have never been cut, their mystery forever preserved, like a bird's folded wing, or a fan never opened.

175. Viva to Louis Waldon, the other fucker in *Blue Movie:*

"We don't want to see your ugly cock and balls . . .
It should be hidden."
Louis: "You can't see it."
Viva: "Well, it should be hidden."

176. This idea has its charms, but I think it possible that I have watched too many blue movies for it to have a lasting hold on me. If you grow accustomed to wall-to-wall, even the slightest shred of mystery or plot can become an agitation. Who cares why these people have found them-

selves in this banal, suburban tract home in Burbank? He is not a delivery man; she is not a bored housewife. They are not the stars—their orifices are. Let them open.

177. Perhaps it is becoming clearer why I felt no romance when you told me that you carried my last letter with you, everywhere you went, for months on end, unopened. This may have served some purpose for you, but whatever it was, surely it bore little resemblance to mine. I never aimed to give you a talisman, an empty vessel to flood with whatever longing, dread, or sorrow happened to be the day's mood. I wrote it because I had something to say to you.

178. Neither Cornell nor Warhol made the mistake of thinking that all desire is yearning. For Warhol, fucking was less about desire than it was about killing time: it is take-it-or-leave-it work, accomplished similarly by geniuses and retards, just like everything else at the Factory. For Cornell, desire was a sharpness, a tear in the static of everyday life—in his diaries he calls it "the spark," "the lift," or "the zest." It delivers not an ache, but a sudden

state of grace. It might be worth noting here that both Warhol and Cornell could arguably be described, at least for periods of their lives, as celibate.

179. When I imagine a celibate man—especially one who doesn't even jerk off—I wonder how he relates to his dick: what else he does with it, how he handles it, how he *regards* it. At first glance, this same question for a woman might appear more "tucked away" (pussy-as-absence, pussy-as-lack: out of sight, out of mind). But I am inclined to think that anyone who thinks or talks this way has simply never felt the pulsing of a pussy in serious need of fucking—a pulsing that communicates nothing less than the suckings and ejaculations of the heart.

180. I have not yet spoken of the princess of blue, which is somewhat intentional: it is unwise to give away too much information about a good dealer, and she has been, for almost two decades now, an excellent and primary supplier of blue. But I will say this: the other night I dreamed of visiting her in her forest. In the dream she was sitting cross-legged, as was I, but she levitated. She wasn't a deity—it was just that I had sought her and was

now her guest. The forest was translucent. We talked. She told me that pollution, too, could be worshiped, simply because it exists. But Eden, she said, there's no Eden. And this forest where we're sitting, it doesn't really exist.

181. *Pharmakon* means drug, but as Jacques Derrida and others have pointed out, the word in Greek famously refuses to designate whether *poison* or *cure*. It holds both in the bowl. In the dialogues Plato uses the word to refer to everything from an illness, its cause, its cure, a recipe, a charm, a substance, a spell, artificial color, and paint. Plato does not call fucking *pharmakon,* but then again, while he talks plenty about love, Plato does not say much about fucking.

182. In the *Phaedrus,* the written word is also notoriously called *pharmakon.* The question up for debate between Socrates and Phaedrus is whether the written word kills memory or aids it—whether it cripples the mind's power, or whether it cures it of its forgetfulness. Given the multiple meanings of *pharmakon,* the answer is, in a sense, a matter of translation.

183. Goethe also worries over the destructive effects of writing. In particular, he worries over how to "keep the essential quality [of the thing] still living before us, and not to kill it with the word." I must admit, I no longer worry much about such things. For better or worse, I do not think that writing changes things very much, if at all. For the most part, I think it leaves everything as it is. *What does your poetry do?*—I guess it gives a kind of blue rinse to the language (John Ashbery).

184. Writing is, in fact, an astonishing equalizer. I could have written half of these propositions drunk or high, for instance, and half sober; I could have written half in agonized tears, and half in a state of clinical detachment. But now that they have been shuffled around countless times —now that they have been made to appear, at long last, running forward as one river—how could either of us tell the difference?

185. Perhaps this is why writing all day, even when the work feels arduous, never feels to me like "a hard day's

work." Often it feels more like balancing two sides of an equation—occasionally quite satisfying, but essentially a hard and passing rain. It, too, kills the time.

186. Another form of aggrandizement: to make a substance into a god, even if one eventually condemns it as a false one. It was in an effort to puncture precisely this sort of embellishment that the French poet Guillaume Apollinaire opted to call his 1913 book of poems not *L'eau de vie*, but the more precise, much "cooler," *Alcools*.

187. Is it a related form of aggrandizement, to inflate a heartbreak into a sort of allegory? Losing what one loves is simpler, more common, than that. More precise. One could leave it, too, as it is. —*Yet how can I explain, that every time I put a pin in the balloon of it, the balloon seems to swell back up as soon as I turn away from it?*

188. How often I've imagined the bubble of body and breath you and I made, even though by now I can hardly remember what you look like, I can hardly see your face.

189. How often, in my private mind, have I choreo-graphed ribbons of black and red in water, two serious ropes of heart and mind. The ink and the blood in the turquoise water: these are the colors inside the fucking.

190. What's past is past. One could leave it as it is, too.

191. On the other hand, it must be admitted that there are aftereffects, impressions that linger long after the external cause has been removed, or has removed itself. "If any-one looks at the sun, he may retain the image in his eyes for several days," Goethe wrote. "Boyle relates an image of ten years." And who is to say this afterimage is not equally real? Indigo makes its stain not in the dyeing vat, but after the garment has been removed. It is the oxygen of the air that blues it.

192. *Cyanosis:* "a blueness of the skin due to imperfectly oxygenated blood, as from a malformation of the heart." As in: "His love for me produces a cyanosis" (S. Judd, 1851).

193. I will admit, however, upon considering the matter further, that writing does do something to one's memory —that at times it can have the effect of an album of childhood photographs, in which each image replaces the memory it aimed to preserve. Perhaps this is why I am avoiding writing about too many specific blue things—I don't want to displace my memories of them, nor embalm them, nor exalt them. In fact, I think I would like it best if my writing could empty me further of them, so that I might become a better vessel for new blue things.

194. One can wish to be surprised (*état d'attente*), but it is hard, if not impossible, to *will* being surprised. Perhaps the most one can do is look back and see that surprises have occurred, chances are that they will again. "Though lovers be lost love shall not," etc. But I am not yet sure how to sever the love from the lover without occasioning some degree of carnage.

195. Does an album of written thoughts perform a similar displacement, or replacement, of the "original" thoughts

themselves? (Please don't start protesting here that there are no thoughts outside of language, which is like telling someone that her colored dreams are, in fact, colorless.) But if writing does displace the idea—if it *extrudes* it, as it were, like grinding a lump of wet clay through a hole— where does the excess go? "We don't want to pollute our world with leftover egos" (Chögyam Trungpa).

196. I suppose I am avoiding writing down too many specific memories of you for similar reasons. The most I will say is "the fucking." Why else suppress the details? Clearly I am not a private person, and quite possibly I am a fool. "Oh, how often have I cursed those foolish pages of mine which made my youthful sufferings public property!" Goethe wrote years after the publication of *The Sorrows of Young Werther.* Sei Shōnagon felt similarly: "Whatever people may think of my book," she wrote after her pillow book gained fame and notoriety, "I still regret that it ever came to light."

197. I suppose it is possible that one day we will meet again and it will feel as if nothing ever happened be-

tween us. This seems unimaginable, but the fact is that it happens all the time. "No whiteness (lost) is so white as the memory / of whiteness," wrote Williams. But one can lose the memory of whiteness, too.

198. In a 1994 interview, about twenty years after he wrote "Famous Blue Raincoat," Cohen admitted that he could no longer remember the specifics of the love triangle that the song describes. "I always felt that there was an invisible male seducing the woman I was with, now whether this one was incarnate or merely imaginary I don't remember." I find this forgetting quite heartening and quite tragic, in turns.

199. For to wish to forget how much you loved someone— and then, to actually forget—can feel, at times, like the slaughter of a beautiful bird who chose, by nothing short of grace, to make a habitat of your heart. I have heard that this pain can be converted, as it were, by accepting "the fundamental impermanence of all things." This accept- ance bewilders me: sometimes it seems an act of will; at

others, of surrender. Often I feel myself to be rocking between them (seasickness).

200. "You cannot step into the same river twice"—a heartening anthem, without a doubt. But really this is but one version of the fragment left behind by Heraclitus, who was justly nicknamed "The Riddler" or "The Obscure." Other versions: "On those stepping into rivers staying the same other and other waters flow"; "We step and do not step into the same river; we are and we are not"; "You cannot step twice into the same river, for other waters and yet others, go flowing on." It seems that *something* is staying the same here, but what?

201. I believe in the possibility—the inevitability, even—of a fresh self stepping into ever-fresh waters, as in the variant: "No man ever steps into the same river twice, for it's not the same river and he's not the same man." But I also sense something in Heraclitus's fragment that allows for the possibility of a mouse shocking its snout on a hunk of electrified cheese over and over again in a kind of static eternity.

202. For the fact is that neuroscientists who study memory remain unclear on the question of whether each time we remember something we are accessing a stable "memory fragment"—often called a "trace" or an "engram"—or whether each time we remember something we are literally creating a new "trace" to house the thought. And since no one has yet been able to discern the *material* of these traces, nor to locate them in the brain, how one thinks of them remains mostly a matter of metaphor: they could be "scribbles," "holograms," or "imprints"; they could live in "spirals," "rooms," or "storage units." Personally, when I imagine my mind in the act of remembering, I see Mickey Mouse in *Fantasia,* roving about in a milky, navy-blue galaxy shot through with twinkling cartoon stars.

203. I remember, in the eighties, when crack first hit the scene, hearing all kinds of horror stories about how if you smoked it even once, the memory of its unbelievable high would live on in your system forever, and you would thus never again be able to be content without it. I have no idea if this is true, but I will admit that it scared me off the

drug. In the years since, I have sometimes found myself wondering if the same principle applies in other realms— if seeing a particularly astonishing shade of blue, for example, or letting a particularly potent person inside you, could alter you irrevocably, just to have seen or felt it. In which case, how does one know when, or how, to refuse? How to recover?

204. Lately I have been trying to learn something about "the fundamental impermanence of all things" from my collection of blue amulets, which I have placed on a ledge in my house that is, for a good half of the day, drenched in sunlight. The placement is intentional—I like to see the sun pass through the blue glass, the bottle of blue ink, the translucent blue stones. But the light is clearly destroying some of the objects, or at least bleaching out their blues. Daily I think about moving the most vulnerable objects to a "cool, dark place," but the truth is that I have little to no instinct for protection. Out of laziness, curiosity, or cruelty—if one can be cruel to objects—I have given them up to their diminishment.

205. One of the most vulnerable items is a scrap of paper
that reads: *you said you think of blue,* written to me by a
lover from long ago. Onto this note he pasted a square of
ripped blue paper, which he then meticulously stitched
back together. The whole apparatus is now falling apart
—the stitches peeling off, the words fading. This seems
just, as this lover was always breaking things then coming
up with ingenious means of rigging them back together.
In each place he lived, he built a bed high in the air served
by a precarious ladder, then placed precious orchids on
wobbly stands near the bottom of the ladder so that often
one would knock the flowers over upon one's descent.
This man had one tattoo, a navy blue snake, which I liked
to watch dance against the white of his wrist when the rest
of his hand had disappeared inside me. He got this tattoo
to commemorate the night that all of his snakes died, a
winter night in Connecticut when it was so cold and the
heat shut off, so he put as many lights as possible against
the snakes' cage to try to keep them warm. Then we fell
asleep and the heat came back on and the snakes over-
heated and died. This was much worse than knocking

over an orchid. This man once taught me how to kill a mouse by thwapping it against the table while holding on to its tail, you do that if the snake strikes and wounds but doesn't kill. It's cruel to keep the mouse alive, he said, just because the snake has lost interest. Eventually he got a new snake, a rainbow boa named Buttercup, a rope of incandescence. Buttercup's colors were a source of endless fascination to me, but she was five feet long and strong and I did not like to feel her coil around my biceps if he wasn't in the room. Near the end, which neither of us quite saw coming, he said he had a surprise for me, and the surprise was another blue tattoo, this one a distorted circle at the base of his neck. It was very beautiful on him, very simple. I didn't live with it long enough to know about what it did.

206. Perhaps writing is not really *pharmakon*, but more of a *mordant*—a means of binding color to its object—or of feeding it into it, like a tattoo needle drumming ink into skin. But "mordant," too, has a double edge: it derives from *mordēre, to bite*—so it is not just a fixative or preserver, but also an acid, a *corrosive*. Did I have this dou-

ble meaning in mind when I told you, a little over a year ago, after it became clear that I would lose you, or that I had already lost you, that you were "etched into my heart"? I may not have known then that "etch" derives from *etzen* or *ezjan—to be eaten*—but in the days since, I have come to know the full meaning of the root.

207. I can remember a time when I took Henry James's advice—"Try to be one of the people on whom nothing is lost!"—deeply to heart. I think I was then imagining that the net effect of becoming one of those people would always be one of *accretion*. Whereas if you truly become someone on whom nothing is lost, then loss will not be lost upon you, either.

208. Cornell's diary entry for February 28, 1947: "Resolve this day as before to transcend in my work the overwhelming sense of sadness that has been so binding and wasteful in past."

209. Duras did not think of alcohol as a false god, but rather as a kind of placeholder, a squatter in the space

made by God's absence. "Alcohol doesn't console," she wrote. "All it replaces is the lack of God." It does not necessarily follow, however, that if and when a substance vacates the spot (renunciation), God rushes in to fill it. For some, the emptiness itself is God; for others, the space must stay empty. "Lots of space, nothing holy": one Zen master's definition of enlightenment (Bodhidharma).

210. For Emerson, dreams and drunkenness were but the "semblance and counterfeit" of an "oracular genius." Therein lies their danger: they mimic—often quite well—the "flames and generosities of the heart." I suppose he is advocating, in his "sermons," which steadily displace the God of theology with one of Nature, what we might now term "a natural high."

211. But are you sure—one would like to ask—that it really is mimicry, *fumisterie?* —Well, don't ask, but look. Look for yourself, and ask not what has been real and what has been false, but what has been bitter, and what has been sweet.

212. If I were today on my deathbed, I would name my love of the color blue and making love with you as two of the sweetest sensations I knew on this earth.

213. But are you certain—one would like to ask—that it was sweet?

214. —No, not really, or not always. If I am to enforce a rule of "brutal honesty," perhaps not even often.

215. It often happens that we treat pain as if it were the only real thing, or at least the *most* real thing: when it comes round, everything before it, around it, and, perhaps, in front of it, tends to seem fleeting, delusional. Of all the philosophers, Schopenhauer is the most hilarious and direct spokesperson for this idea: "As a rule we find pleasure much less pleasurable, pain much more painful than we expected." You don't believe him? He offers this quick test: "Compare the feelings of an animal engaged in eating another with those of the animal being eaten."

216. Today is the fifth anniversary, the radio says, of the day on which "everything changed." It says this so often that I turn it off. *Everything changed. Everything changed.* Well, what changed? What did the blade reveal? For whom did it come? "I grieve that grief can teach me nothing," wrote Emerson.

217. "We're only given as much as the heart can endure," "What does not kill you makes you stronger," "Our sorrows provide us with the lessons we most need to learn": these are the kinds of phrases that enrage my injured friend. Indeed, one would be hard-pressed to come up with a spiritual lesson that demands becoming a quadriparalytic. The tepid "there must be a reason for it" notion sometimes floated by religious or quasi-religious acquaintances or bystanders, is, to her, another form of violence. She has no time for it. She is too busy asking, in this changed form, what makes a livable life, and how she can live it.

218. As her witness, I can testify to no reason, no lesson. But I can say this: in watching her, sitting with her, help-

ing her, weeping with her, touching her, and talking with her, I have seen the bright pith of her soul. I cannot tell you what it looks like, exactly, but I can say that I have seen it.

219. Likewise, I can say that seeing it has made me a believer, though I cannot say what, or in what, exactly, I have come to believe.

220. Imagine someone saying, "Our fundamental situation is joyful." Now imagine *believing* it.

221. Or forget belief: imagine *feeling*, even if for a moment, that it were true.

222. In January 2002, camping in the Dry Tortugas, on an island which is essentially an abandoned fort ninety miles north of Cuba, flipping through a copy of *Nature* magazine. I read that the color of the universe (whatever this might mean—here I gather that it means the result of a survey of the spectrum of light emitted by around 200,000 galaxies) has finally been deduced. The color of

the universe, the article says, is "pale turquoise." *Of course,* I think, looking out wistfully over the glittering Gulf. *I knew it all along. The heart of the world is blue.*

223. A few months later, back at home, I read somewhere else that this result was in error, due to a computer glitch. The *real* color of the universe, this new article says, is light beige.

224. Recently I found out that "les bluets" can translate as "cornflowers." You might think I would have known this all along, as I have been calling this book "Bluets" (mispronounced) for years. But somehow I had only ever heard, "a small blue flower with a yellow center that grows abundantly in the countryside of France." I thought I'd never seen it.

225. Shortly after finding out about the bluets, I have a dream in which I am sent an abundance of cornflowers. In this dream it is perfectly all right that that is their name. They do not need to be bluets any longer. They are American, they are shaggy, they are wild, they are strong. They

do not signify romance. They were sent by no one in celebration of nothing. I had known them all along.

226. As I collected blues for this project—in folders, in boxes, in notebooks, in memory—I imagined creating a blue tome, an encyclopedic compendium of blue observations, thoughts, and facts. But as I lay out my collection now, what strikes me most is its *anemia*—an anemia that seems to stand in direct proportion to my zeal. I thought I had collected enough blue to build a mountain, albeit one of detritus. But it seems to me now as if I have stumbled upon a pile of thin blue gels scattered on the stage long after the show has come and gone; the set, striked.

227. Perhaps this is as it should be. Wittgenstein's *Tractatus Logico-Philosophicus*—the first and only book of philosophy he published in his lifetime—clocks in at sixty pages, and offers a grand total of seven propositions. "As to the shortness of the book I am *awfully sorry for it; but what can I do?*" he wrote to his translator. "If you were to squeeze me like a lemon you would get nothing more out of me."

228. My injured friend is now able to write letters via voice-recognition software to keep her friends abreast of changes in her condition, of which there have been many. "My life can change, *does* change," she asserts—and it has, and does, often in astonishing ways. Nonetheless, near the end of these letters, she usually includes a short paragraph that acknowledges her ongoing physical pain, and her intense grief for all she has lost, a grief she describes as bottomless. "If I did not write of the difficulties under which I labor, I would fear to be misrepresenting the grinding reality of quadriplegia and spinal cord injury," she says. "So here it is, the paragraph that roundly asserts that I continue to suffer."

229. I am writing all this down in blue ink, so as to remember that all words, not just some, are written in water.

230. Holed up in the north country for the month of May, a May which saw but four days of sunshine. The rest of the month was solid gray, drizzling or pouring rain, rendering everything green. Rushing and verdant. In short, a nightmare. Each day I took long walks in my yellow poncho, looking for blue, for any blue thing. I found only

tarps (always tarps!) pinned over stacks of firewood, a few blue recycling containers kicked over in the streets, a grayish blue mailbox here and there. I came back to my dark chamber each night empty-eyed, empty-handed, as if I had been panning fruitlessly for gold all day in a cold river. *Stop working against the world,* I counseled myself. *Love the one you're with. Love the color green.* But I did not love the green, nor did I want to have to love it or pretend to love it. The most I can say is that I abided it.

231. That month I touched myself every night in my narrow bed and came thinking of you, knowing all the while that I was planting the seeds of a fresh disaster. The disaster did not come then, but it did come later. "Though six days smoothly run, / The seventh will bring blue devils or a dun" (Byron, 1823). The most I can say is that this time I learned my lesson. I stopped hoping.

232. Perhaps, in time, I will also stop missing you.

233. That the future is unknowable is, for some, God's means of suturing us in, or to, the present moment. For others, it is the mark of a malevolence, a sure sign that our

entire existence here is best understood as a sort of joke or mistake.

234. For me, it is neither. It is simply the way that it is. Whether this accident be a happy or unhappy one is probably more a matter of mood than anything else; the difficulty is that "our moods do not believe in each other" (Emerson). One can wander about the landscape looking for clues, amassing evidence, but even the highest pile never seems to decide the case.

235. "One thing they don't tell you 'bout the blues when you got 'em, you keep on fallin' 'cause there ain't no bottom," sings Emmylou Harris, and she may be right. Perhaps it would help to be told that there is no bottom, save, as they say, wherever and whenever you stop digging. You have to stand there, spade in hand, cold whiskey sweat beaded on your brow, eyes misshapen and wild, some sorry-ass grave digger grown bone-tired of the trade. You have to stand there in the dirty rut you dug, alone in the darkness, in all its pulsing quiet, surrounded by the scandal of corpses.

236. Do not be overly troubled by this fact. "Nine days out of ten," wrote Merleau-Ponty of Cézanne, "all he saw around him was the wretchedness of his empirical life and of his unsuccessful attempts, the debris of an unknown celebration."

237. In any case, I am no longer counting the days.

238. I want you to know, if you ever read this, there was a time when I would rather have had you by my side than any one of these words; I would rather have had you by my side than all the blue in the world.

239. But now you are talking as if love were a consolation. Simone Weil warned otherwise. "Love is not consolation," she wrote. "It is light."

240. All right then, let me try to rephrase. When I was alive, I aimed to be a student not of longing but of light.

(2003–2006)

Credits

THE PRINCIPAL CORRESPONDENTS

Rebecca Baron, Joshua Beckman, Brian Blanchfield (aka Student Blue), Mike Bryant, Lap-Chi Chu, Christina Crosby, Cort Day, Annie Dillard, Doug Goodwin, George Hambrecht, Christian Hawkey, Wayne Koestenbaum, Aaron Kunin, PJ Mark (aka Balarama), Anthony McCann, Sean Nevin, Martín Plot, Janet Sarbanes, Mady Schutzman, Matthew Sharpe, Craig Tracy (who supplied the ink), and my dearest Harry (who brought the light).

THE PRINCIPAL SUPPLIERS

Ludwig Wittgenstein, Philosophical Investigations, *trans. G. E. M. Anscombe; Johann Wolfgang von Goethe,* Theory of Colours, trans. *Charles Lock Eastlake.*

OTHER SUPPLIERS

American Folk Art Museum; David Batchelor, Chromophobia; *Victoria Finlay,* Color: A Natural History of the Palette; *John Gage,* Color and Culture: Practice and Meaning from Antiquity to Abstraction; *Michel Pastoureau,* Blue: The History of a Color; *Patrick Trevor-Roper,* The World through Blunted Sight; The Stanford Encyclopedia of Philosophy *(online); Vermont Studio Center.*

OTHER APPEARANCES

Some of these propositions first appeared, in various forms, in Black Clock, The Canary, The Hat, *and* MiPOesias. *Grateful acknowledgment to their editors.*

For Lily Mazzarella
first and forever
princess of blue.

BIOGRAPHY

Maggie Nelson is most recently the author of Women, the New York School, and Other True Abstractions *(University of Iowa Press, 2007; winner of the 2008 Susanne M. Glasscock Humanities Book Prize for Interdisciplinary Scholarship) and* The Red Parts: A Memoir *(Free Press, 2007; named a Notable Book of the Year by the State of Michigan). She is also the author of several books of poetry, including* Something Bright, Then Holes *(Soft Skull Press, 2007), and* Jane: A Murder *(Soft Skull, 2005; finalist, the PEN/Martha Albrand Award for the Art of the Memoir). A recipient of a Creative Capital/Andy Warhol Foundation Arts Writers Grant, she currently teaches on the faculty of the School of Critical Studies at CalArts in Valencia, California, and lives in Los Angeles.*